The H

A play

By

Patrick Prior

Inspired by a short story by Edward Bulwer Lytton

Strumpet Books

The Haunters was first performed at the Yvonne Arnaud, Mill Studio,

Guildford, in 2002 with the following cast:

DR WILLIAMS...Pat Abernethy

MR BOWERS...Dave Marsden

Written by PATRICK PRIOR

Directed by JIM DUNK

The play has subsequently been performed at many venues in the UK

including:

Brewhouse Theatre, Taunton

Middlesbrough Theatre

Palace Theatre, Newark

Wilde Theatre, Bracknell

Adam Smith Theatre, Kirkcaldy

Rose Theatre, Kidderminster

Ellen Terry Theatre, Kent

ACT ONE

THE TIME: LATE. 19TH CENTURY.

The stage is almost bare. Props are minimal, perhaps a couple of chairs, a table and one or two packing cases. Settings are created mainly with light and sound. As the house lights dim, over the sound system a woman crying softly echoes faintly. The darkness is held for a couple of beats. Only the crying is heard. As the play goes up, a coffin, resting on a bier, is seen lit in a pool of light. The crying bleeds into the scene for a few seconds before fading away. A man enters. He carries a wreath. This is Mr Bowers, a lawyer. He places the wreath on top of the coffin. He makes a tender gesture, almost touching the coffin. He then gathers himself and walks purposefully into the darkness. Dr Williams enters. He stands by the coffin.

DR WILLIAMS: My brother died. The brother who raised and cared for me, who was mother and father to me. died...

(Light up on Bowers who stands some way off and is giving a eulogy for the dead man)

MR BOWERS: He was only known to me for a little while but in that time I grew to respect his integrity, his honesty and his courage...

DR WILLIAMS: He died a mysterious and terrible death...

MR BOWERS: He was a man of compassion. A man who dedicated his life to the service of others. A man whose flame was all too briefly snuffed out.

(Fade light down on Bowers)

DR WILLIAMS: The news of his death only reached me two weeks after his funeral. I had been in Switzerland trying to recover my health. A weakness of

3

the heart and lungs had led me to seek the clearer purer air of the mountains in an attempt to ease the condition. Because I had been moving from canton to canton, the telegraph reached me too late to attend the burial.

(Fade down light on coffin)

I caught the train from Lucerne and started out on the long journey to London…

(As he speaks the sound of a moving steam train is heard. Lighting suggests the movement of the locomotive)

I wanted to know why my brother was dead. A brother hale and hearty and in the prime of life. As I left Switzerland and my journey took me through France towards Calais the very rhythm of the train seemed to chant those terrible words in the telegram over and over in my head "Brother dead. Return at once. Brother dead Return at Once. Brother dead. Return at once"

If I had known the truth, and of the horrors which awaited me, it would have been better I'd died myself among those beautiful mountains. It would have been better if I'd never been born….

(The sound of the train coming to a halt and the hiss of steam. A train whistle sounds)

Victoria Station. My spirits sink even more as I look around at the drizzling mist which crouches over London in late winter.

(Over the sound system comes the street sounds of Victorian London)

The city hangs its head under the dank, sullen air. Houses and shops send out weak yellow beams of gaslight which seem barely seem able to pierce a few inches into the gloom. Morose horses pull cabs through the grey morning while their drivers sit huddled and miserable against the mist and spiteful rain. I think

4

for a moment of the clear Swiss mountains I've left so recently. This is the real beginning of the story. This is when my journey to the truth of my brother's death is to begin. This is where my terror is to begin…

(He checks a piece of paper as if looking for an address. The sounds of street life are still heard)

The name at the bottom of the telegraphic message is that of Mr Bowers, solicitor. The address given is in Oxford Street. I find the entrance to the office, mount the stairs and enter.

(The sounds of the street have faded away as light comes up on Bowers sitting reading some legal documents)

Mr Bowers? Your clerk told me to come in.

MR BOWERS: Dr Williams? Please, sir, take a seat.

(Dr Williams sits down)

DR WILLIAMS: Thank you.

(He coughs)

MR BOWERS: Are you alright, Dr Williams? Can I get you something? Some tea? A brandy perhaps?

DR WILLIAMS: No. No. I'll be alright in moment. A weakness of the lungs. I'm not used to the London air.

MR BOWERS: Yes. Yes. The weather has been dreadful the last week or two. We've had endless rain, then the usual fogs of course. Are you sure you don't want anything to drink, Dr Williams?

DR WILLIAMS: Very sure.

MR BOWERS: May I take this opportunity, sir, to convey my very deepest sympathies on your sad news. In the short time I knew your brother I came to respect him. His death came as a dreadful shock to us all. A dreadful shock.

DR WILLIAMS: Thank you. Your telegraphic message, it didn't say much beyond the bare fact.

MR BOWERS: Yes, well, I...I find that any...sensitive information should be quite properly kept confidential and only divulged to the person, or persons concerned. I hope you understand.

DR WILLIAMS: Yes, yes of course. Well, Mr Bowers, perhaps you can now enlighten me as to how my brother died?

MR BOWERS: Right. Are you sure you wouldn't like a brandy, Dr Williams?

DR WILLIAMS: No thank you.

MR BOWERS: Would you mind if I...?

(He nods to indicate the brandy)

DR WILLIAMS: Please.

(Bowers pours a brandy)

MR BOWERS: Oh dear, telling you this is rather...

(He takes a drink of brandy)

...telling you this is rather...What I mean is, Dr Williams, is that you may find this distressing. Are you sure a brandy...?

DR WILLIAMS: Mr Bowers, I'm a doctor. Human misery's not new to me. However distressing the news I can assure you I would prefer to hear it straight and without any molly-coddling.

MR BOWERS: Very well, sir. Your brother took his own life.

DR WILLIAMS: Took…? No. No. That's not possible. That's nonsense! Robert was the last man on earth to take his own life! There's been some sort of mistake.

MR BOWERS: No mistake, I'm afraid, sir. Your brother died by his own hand.

DR WILLIAMS: How?

MR BOWERS: He… cut his throat.

(Dr Williams coughs again, this time more violently)

Tsk. Tsk. Tsk. My dear sir. My dear sir.

(He pours a brandy and hands it to Dr Williams)

Here, take it, please. It will help.

(Dr Williams takes a gulp of the brandy and the coughing subsides)

DR WILLIAMS: Thank you. Shock it…can trigger the condition.

MR BOWERS: Try a little more brandy.

DR WILLIAMS: No. No, thank you. I'm alright now. I've had enough.

(He hands the remainder of the brandy to Mr Bowers)

 I'd be obliged if you would give me the details, Mr Bowers.

MR BOWERS: Oh, well, waste not want not.

(He drinks the rest of the brandy in Dr William's glass)

Some weeks ago your brother, your *late* brother, rented a house. In east London. Limehouse to be precise. He engaged me to act on his behalf in the transaction. The house had been empty for some time. Your brother told me that he intended to set up a practice there, using part of the house as a dispensary for the poor. He moved his possessions in and decided to work whilst the house was being renovated. It was only three days after taking up residence it happened. Your brother was found on the front doorstep of the house… He…he had slashed his own throat. The razor was still in his hand. I'm so sorry to be the bearer of such awful tidings, Dr Williams.

DR WILLIAMS: You say he was found on the doorstep?

MR BOWERS: Yes. One of the workmen arriving that morning raised the alarm. Nothing could be done.

DR WILLIAMS: But it doesn't make sense? Even if Robert did want to die that way why would he do it at the front door? Why not in a bedroom? A bathroom?

MR BOWERS: It was surmised by the coroner that in the act of shaving the doctor had been seized by a fit of temporary madness and took his own life while the balance of his mind was disturbed.

DR WILLIAMS: Just a moment, Mr Bowers. Are you saying my brother suddenly decided to kill himself while shaving?

MR BOWERS: When the body…when your brother was found, Dr Williams, he was still in his shirt sleeves and still had traces of lather about his face. So it was naturally assumed that the fit which unhinged his mind occurred while he was shaving.

DR WILLIAMS: Let me ask you something, Mr Bowers. If you stood at a shaving mirror and decided to cut your own throat would you run through the house, open the front door and do it on the doorstep? Would you?

MR BOWERS: No. Put like that, of course not. But it is possible that the doctor after…injuring himself may have come to his senses and been running for help. He could have then collapsed at the front door through loss of blood.

DR WILLIAMS: Then I take it there was a trail of blood through the house to the front door?

MR BOWERS: Hrumph. As far as I'm aware there was no blood inside the house itself, no.

DR WILLIAMS: Then it's logical to assume that the injury actually took place on the front doorstep which leads me back to my original point. Why would a man intending to cut his own throat run through the house and do it on the front doorstep?

MR BOWERS: Doctor Williams, I must admit I'm as puzzled as you are about how your brother came to be where he was. But the coroner saw no evidence of foul play and however the circumstances came about there's no doubt the poor man took his own life. I really am sorry.

DOCTOR WILLIAMS: Thank you.

(There is a momentary silence)

MR BOWERS: Your brother, he spoke of you quite a lot. He was very proud of you being a physician.

DR WILLIAMS: Was he? If the truth be told, Mr Bowers, it was because Robert was a doctor I took up medicine. He was…he was a sort of hero to me, I suppose. When our parents died I was only…what?…ten? Robert was eight years older. Cholera. They died of Cholera. We were sent to live with an elderly aunt in Highgate. She gave us a roof over our heads, fed us and clothed us. But it was really Robert who brought me up. He was a great man, Mr Bowers, a great man.

MR BOWERS: Yes, I can believe that. I know that this isn't the most sensitive of times to bring up the subject of your brother's estate, Doctor Williams, and I am aware of your own deep feelings of grief, but would you mind if I briefly outline the legal position?

DR WILLIAMS: What? No. No, of course not, Mr Bowers. I suppose it has to be done sometime.

MR BOWERS: As the only living relative you. of course, inherit the estate in its entirety. This includes two thousand pounds in cash, and a number of stocks to the value of seven hundred and fifty pounds.

DR WILLIAMS: I didn't know Robert was so circumspect with money. When he was younger it ran through his fingers like water.

MR BOWERS: However, there are many items in the house itself, personal belongings, correspondence, medical supplies and equipment, which have not been inventoried. They are yours, naturally. Perhaps we could go down to the house and I could show you the goods and chattel? Would tomorrow be convenient, Doctor Williams?

(Doctor Williams is lost in his own thoughts)

Doctor Williams?

DR WILLIAMS: Sorry. I…eh…You were saying, Mr Bowers?

MR BOWERS: About tomorrow. If we could go down and check the residue of the estate?

DR WILLIAMS: Fine.

MR BOWERS: Right. Good. If you could call here, shall we say at eleven o'clock, then we can go down there together.

(He holds out his hand. They shake)

Till tomorrow, then, Doctor Williams.

(Doctor Williams walks to the door. As he leaves the office the lights fade down on Mr Bowers who resumes reading the legal documents. The sounds of the street are heard)

DR WILLIAMS: Oxford Street goes about its business as I leave the office. Packed humanity bumps and bores against me as I walk along the pavement in a daze. Thoughts whirl and dance in my head. My brother is dead. He died in a pool of blood, a razor in his hand. My heart beats wildly. My breath catches in my chest. I want everyone to stop. I want everyone mourn. It's only when personal tragedy strikes and the world carries on unconcernedly that we realise how little we all matter. I blindly walk on towards my lodgings in Holborn. I remember almost nothing of my journey. I just want to be alone.

(Fade down street sounds. The chiming of a clock is heard as Dr Williams sits in a chair in his study)

It's twelve o'clock. Sleep is impossible. So I sit here in my study, going over Robert's death. I cannot accept the version I have been given. Every instinct tells me that something is wrong. I read over some of the letters my brother sent me while I was abroad, they only serve to confirm my doubts...

(As he looks at the letters, over the sound system comes echoing fragments of his brother's writings)

ROBERT/ON SOUND SYSTEM: Dear Little Brother, Exciting news. I have found my direction in life at last...Dear Little Brother, I trust all goes as well with you as it does with me. Within the next few weeks I hope to have things settled and begin my plans at last...Dear Little Brother. I'm so glad your health is on the mend. I have such great hopes for your return...Dear Little Brother, All is almost complete. I keep it as a surprise for your return but our dream of working as physicians together may at last begin. What a difference we shall make...

(Extracts from the letters revolve and echo is his head)

...found my direction in life at last....what a difference we shall make...dear little brother...begin my plans at last...such great hopes....within a few weeks...such great hopes...all goes well...exciting news...almost complete...dear little brother...

(The words overlap in a jumble of phrases. The voice gets louder and louder)

...greathopeswhatadifferencedirectionatlastgreathopesmyplansatlastgreathopesg reathopesgreathopes...

(As the sound reaches a climax Doctor Williams lets out a great cry of anguish. There is a sudden silence, only broken by the ticking of the clock)

DR WILLIAMS: The letters, the letters only sent to me a few weeks before he died told me not of a man who was looking for death, but a man in love with life. How could he change so much so quickly? What made him die so terribly? Perhaps the place of his death holds the answer...

(He gets out of the chair)

It's now morning. A watery sun's managed to shed its light on the city for a few hours. Mr Bowers and I meet at his office and catch an omnibus to Limehouse.

(Bring up sound of horse-drawn omnibus. Bring up light on Bowers who sways with the movement of the carriage. Dr Williams sits beside him)

As the morning is unusually fine we grab the chance to get some fresh air and sun, so we take seats on the open top deck. From my vantage point I can see the west end unfold as the omnibus makes its way along the Strand towards the City of London.

MR BOWERS: The house itself is about a seventy years old, Doctor Williams. I believe it was built for one of the rich merchant families who made their fortune in trade. It stands quite close to the river. No doubt they wanted to keep a close eye on their investments. This has resulted in a tendency to dampness in the walls at times. I did point this out to your late brother but he didn't seem too perturbed. A nip of brandy to keep out the cold, Dr Williams?

(He produces a hip flask. Doctor Williams shakes his head)

Your health, sir.

(Mr Bowers takes a swig from the flask)

DR WILLIAMS: We've passed through the City and are now in the east end. In a matter of yards the opulence and richness falls away and the streets become an endless stream of dilapidation and despair.

(Bring up street noises of the east end)

Common lodging houses and pubs spill out dirt and noise. The hopeless inhabitants of these places stand around the doorways, their faces mirroring all the vicissitudes and misery of their lives.

MR BOWERS: My word, sir, the sights in this part of London are not pleasant. Not pleasant.

DR WILLIAMS: Men sprawl on the wet pavements, senseless with drink or want. Street woman, gaunt and vulpine, smile up at me in a ghastly parody of sexual attraction...

MR BOWERS: ...But then, of course, the property is, how shall I put it, a difficult rent. Since the last owners left some five years ago there have been numerous attempts to let it out. There does seem to have been an inordinate number of tenants. Most seem to have lasted only a short time before leaving. Some, indeed, have only lived in the house one night...

(Sounds of the east end streets become louder)

DR WILLIAMS: As we near Limehouse the noises and the smells become almost unbearable. Traders bawl out the virtues of the cheap wares festooned over the stalls and barrows which line each side of the road.

MR BOWERS: *(Puts a handkerchief to his face)* My word. That stench really is disgusting.

DR WILLIAMS: The stink of rotting vegetables and fish and the musty aroma of damp clothing drift up. The omnibus stops and Mr Bowers indicates that this is where we get off.

(The clip clop of the omnibus receding into the distance is heard above the street sounds)

MR BOWERS: We can walk from here, Dr Williams. The house is nearer the river.

DR WILLIAMS: Is the churchyard nearby, Mr Bowers? I should like to…

MR BOWERS: Pay your respects? Of course. Of course. As I said on our way here, as you were abroad when the unfortunate…occurrence took place I took the liberty of arranging for your brother to rest in the cemetery in the church grounds. There was some difficulty. Apparently the ecclesiastical authorities are not happy to bury suicides in consecrated ground. I did manage to talk the vicar round. A generous donation to the church fund helped I think, and fortunately he also likes a drop of brandy. However if you should wish that another resting place is more appropriate then I'm sure we…

DR WILLIAMS: No, that's fine, Mr Bowers. Fine.

(The sounds of the street fades away as they walk towards the shadowy and misty churchyard. They reach the graveside. Mr Bowers takes off his hat and bows his head. A church bell tolls)

DR WILLIAMS: My brother's resting place. The earth is still freshly wounded. The flowers are rotted. I try to make a connection between this pile of sad ground and the brother I remember.

(Over the sound system echoes the wailing of children. Doctor Williams looks around as the sound fades away)

MR BOWERS: Is there something wrong, Doctor Williams?

DR WILLIAMS: No. I thought…it was nothing.

(He picks up a handful of earth and throws it on the grave as he does so the sound of the children wailing echoes faintly again)

Did you hear that, Mr Bowers?

MR BOWERS: Hear what?

Doctor Williams: That! There's children crying nearby.

(He looks about)

You must be able to hear them now, surely!

MR BOWERS: I can't hear anything, sir. Honestly!

DOCTOR WILLIAMS: It's coming from that direction. Children. In distress.

(He moves towards the sound)

Hello. Hello. Can we help?

MR BOWERS: Doctor. I don't think there's anybody…

DR WILLIAMS: Of course there is, man! Are you deaf? There are children cry…

(The sounds fade away)

There are children… It's stopped. There was crying. I distinctly heard crying.

MR BOWERS: Sometimes the ships horns from the river can sound quite strange, perhaps…

DR WILLIAMS: It was crying. Children crying! I know the difference, sir, between that and a ship's horn!

MR BOWERS: Of course. Of course.

DR WILLIAMS: I...eh...I do apologise for my rudeness, Mr Bowers. Please forgive me. I'm perhaps more overwrought than I first thought.

MR BOWERS: Think nothing of it, I understand perfectly. Shall we go on to the house?

(Fade down on Mr Bowers. Doctor Williams stands alone in a pool of light)

DOCTOR WILLIAMS: We leave the cemetery and walk down a narrow lane which runs alongside the church. Immediately we're plunged into a labyrinth of mean alleyways and wretched streets. As we near the Thames the feeling of chill grows and the river mist grows thicker, curling about the posts and doorways. Even Mr Bowers, despite several pulls at the brandy flask, seems ill at ease.

MR BOWERS: *(Taking a swig of brandy. He then offers the flask to Dr Williams))* Doctor?

DR WILLIAMS: No thank you.

MR BOWERS: My word, this chill gets into the bones.

(He peers into the fog)

Ah, I think we're there. Come along, Doctor Williams.

(He strides into the fog)

DR WILLIAMS: Suddenly, through a break in the fog stands the house where my brother died. It sits sombre and silent. The leprous walls show the wear and tear of many years. The windows are barred and shuttered, and so the house stares sightlessly at the river only a few hundred yards away.

(Over the sound system comes the melancholy noise of a ship's foghorn)

Here, the mist seems ever thicker and tries to climb the stout wall which completely encircle the house.

(The squeal of a rusty gate being opened is heard)

Mr Bower's pushes open the tall wrought iron gates and we step into the grounds.

(Light up on Mr Bowers who stands in the swirling river mist. He is joined by Doctor Williams)

MR BOWERS: The house has its own quite substantial grounds. Three quarters of an acre I believe. Of course the garden needs a little pruning. Some weeding. But you can still see the original shape, if you look very carefully. Shall we go inside?

(Fade down light on Mr Bowers and Dr Williams. Light up on a couple of packing cases and some odds and ends scattered around the almost empty house. The light is filtering through some partly shuttered windows. The echoing wail of a child briefly reverberates before dying away. Mr Bowers and Dr Williams step into the room. Voices have the faint echoing quality heard when a house is unoccupied)

MR BOWERS: Well, as you can see the house is still pretty tumbledown. These cases are part of your late brother's estate so feel free to check their contents at your convenience.

(He looks around the room)

My word. The place is even less salubrious than I remember from my first visit with your brother. I suggested then he should take some comfortable lodgings until the house was more habitable, but he was in a fine mood to get started so...

I do apologise about the lack of lighting. The shutters haven't been properly removed yet. There should be a lantern or two around somewhere. I'll just see if they've been left in any of the adjoining rooms. Excuse me.

(He exits)

DR WILLIAMS: The room smells mouldy. Dirt clings to everything. Cobwebs criss-cross high up in the corners of the room. On the floor the dust is deep. Footprints are held there. The footprints of how many people? How many years? Robert's must be among them. He must have passed this very way. Perhaps stood where I'm standing now. Are some of these footprints the very marks he made on his way to the front door? On his way to the front door with a razor in his hand? My heart beats with an unnatural rhythm. I must be careful. I mustn't allow my illness to find me here. Not here.

(Over the sound system echoes a brief snatch of indistinct rapid whispering from many voices)

Hello? Mr Bowers?

(The whispering sounds again from another direction, causing him to spin around)

Who's there? Is that you, Mr Bowers?

(Doctor Williams waits for a few seconds. From afar comes the sound of ship's horn on the river He bends down and picks up the charred fragment of a book)

By the fireplace, the remnants of a book. Charred to almost nothing. Even by the fragment left it's obviously been richly bound. A melted fastening, the remains of a lock perhaps. A locked book. A diary. The pages are nothing but ash. The top corner of one or two pages are the only bits left. A few words. Faint and almost illegible in the poor light. The writing to me seems to be in a woman's hand.

(He holds the book at an angle which may catch the light. Over the sound system echoes a woman's voice)

WOMAN ON SOUND SYSTEM: We ought to love…if all was known…

DOCTOR WILLIAMS: "We ought to love…if all was known…" The random words mean nothing, make no sense, yet I am uneasy at reading them.

(The indistinct whispering of many voices echoes again)

Who's there? Mr Bowers?

(The whispering is interspersed with low malevolent chuckling)

If this is someone trespassing then I shall make sure the proper authorities are sent for! Come on. Show yourself! Mr Bowers?

(The pattering of feet is heard softly in the darkness)

I know someone is there!

(The pattering is heard again. Doctor Williams moves towards it Tension music under))

Come on, now. Come on.

(The whispering becomes louder. The laughter echoes chillingly. Tension grows as he moves towards the shadows. Tinkle of tension music rises as he reaches into the shadows. Suddenly a figure looms out at him from the dark. Doctor Williams reels back with. shock. Mr Bowers appears. Doctor Williams is obviously struggling for breath)

MR BOWERS: I do beg your pardon, Doctor. I didn't mean to… Are you alright? Shall I fetch you a glass of water? Something stronger?

(Doctor Williams slowly regains his composure)

DR WILLIAMS: No. No, I'm alright. I'm alright. Just a bit… I heard voices.

MR BOWERS: Someone outside, perhaps.

DOCTOR WILLIAMS: Yes, that's probably it. Someone outside.

MR BOWERS: Are you sure you're alright, Doctor Williams? You look quite pale.

DR WILLIAMS: Yes, fine. Fine.

MR BOWERS: Nevertheless, I think we should go. I couldn't find any lanterns and it's quite impossible to see anything properly. I'll arrange to have some delivered and also try to have the shutters removed by tomorrow. We can do a proper inventory then. To be honest, Doctor Williams, this not the most easy of places to be. I must confess I'm always...relieved to leave. Oh, know that sounds silly but...

(He shivers a little)

Brrrr. The cold is getting into my bones. Why don't we make our way back to the city? We'll go to my club. They do a fine pork chop dinner. A cigar and a glass or two of...

DR WILLIAMS: Brandy?

MR BOWERS: Yes, well why not? Shall we?

(He indicates that they should leave and exits. The church clock chimes three)

Three o' clock. How time flies. Well, let's get off, Doctor. The brandy and pork chops await.

(He exits)

DR WILLIAMS: Already the house is being cloaked in deep shadows
My brother died not twenty feet from where I stand. In this house. In this strange dark house. I must know why. I *will* know why.

(He looks around and pulls his coat tighter about himself. Mr Bowers reappears)

MR BOWERS: Doctor?

(They both exit. In the empty house the soft crying of a woman. echoes. Fade down light in house. Light up on Mr Bowers and Doctor Williams at the club. They sit as if in front of a roaring fire, their faces lit by the dancing flames. Each hold a brandy glass in their hands. The sound of the woman crying bleeds briefly into the scene before fading away.

MR BOWERS: Aaaah. That's better. Tell me this, and tell me true, Doctor Williams, did you ever eat a better dinner than that?

DR WILLIAMS: I can't say I have, Mr Bowers.

MR BOWERS: I thought not. Feeling better?

DR WILLIAMS: How do you mean?

MR BOWERS: After our trip. To the house. You looked rather ill.

DR WILLIAMS: Yes. Quite well, thank you. As I said before, the London air, it doesn't agree with my lungs.

MR BOWERS: Well, I'm not a doctor, but as far as you can't beat a glass or six of brandy for keeping the heart pumping and the lungs blowing. What do you think, sir?

DR WILLIAMS: I'm sure you're right, Mr Bowers.

MR BOWERS: Mind you, a couple of hours in that house is more than enough to make any of us feel ill.

DR WILLIAMS: How do you mean?

MR BOWERS: There's no doubt it's a rum sort of place. I must admit I'm happier coming away from the house than going to it.

DR WILLIAMS: The house disturbs you?

MR BOWERS: Disturbs me? Oh, I'm not sure I'd go as far as saying it disturbs me, I am a lawyer after all. The only thing that disturbs lawyers generally is nonpayment of fees. It's not so much disturbs me as there's a sort of feeling about the place…not…welcoming, if you know that I mean.

DR WILLIAMS: On the omnibus, on the way down to the house this morning you said something about the place 'being a difficult rent'.

MR BOWERS: Did I?

DR WILLIAMS: Yes you did. You said it was difficult to keep tenants. That some only stayed a day or two.

MR BOWERS: Some even less than a day or two. The truth is that for the past five years the turnover of tenants has been unusually high in that particular property.

DR WILLIAMS: Did my brother know this?

MR BOWERS: Oh, yes. Yes, I told him immediately he showed an interest in the house.

DR WILLIAMS: And what was his reaction?

MR BOWERS: He didn't seem to care one way or the other. He said the house and its location was perfect for his needs. Then he signed the lease. He moved in and three days later…well, you know what happened next, sir.

DR WILLIAMS: Mr Bowers, can I ask you something?

MR BOWERS: Of course.

DR WILLIAMS: Why do you think nobody stays in that house for very long?

MR BOWERS: Hrrumph. It's difficult to be precise. There is the problem of damp. And the nearness of the river makes the location unhealthy. Then of course…

DR WILLIAMS: Mr Bowers. These are problems associated with half the houses in London. I ask you now, not as a lawyer, but as one man to another, what do you think is wrong with the house?

MR BOWERS: *(He takes a gulp of brandy)* There's…there's whispers…stories associated with the place. Old wives tales. Things that go bump in the night. You know the sort thing.

DR WILLIAMS: And what do you think of those stories?

MR BOWERS: If you're asking me do I believe them, no sir, I do not. But if you asked me to spend a night alone in that house, I wouldn't do it for a thousand pounds.

(Fade down firelight. Doctor Williams sits alone in the dying red glow)

DR WILLIAMS: Mr Bowers leaves. I sit alone still trying to make sense of the things that've happened. The mystery of my brother's death grows murkier, not clearer. The house with the strange reputation. I'm a man of science such nonsense has no effect on me yet there's no doubt that there is an atmosphere in that place. The voices and cries, they are from a human agency no doubt. But is it merely the peculiarity of the location that makes sound carry? Or is it someone trying to frighten me? I will not be frightened away. I owe the truth whatever it is to my poor dead brother.

(Over the sound system echoes a woman's voice)

WOMAN ON SOUND SYSTEM: We ought to love…if all was known…

DR WILLIAMS: The words in the burned diary they pop into my mind unbidden. A few echoes of the past. They have nothing to tell me I'm sure, yet…

(Over the sound system comes the sound of a hansom cab. The firelight changes to one of movement. Doctor Williams sways with the motion)

It's the next morning. I'm on my way to Limehouse by hansom cab. The chill weather and signs of thickening fog make the omnibus a less pleasant prospect. I've sent a note to Mr Bowers asking me to join me down there later rather than us meeting and travelling together.

(Light up on Mr Bowers who sits at his desk writing)

MR BOWERS: *(He calls off)* Nesbit, when Doctor Williams arrives show him in immediately, will you?

(Fade down on Mr Bowers)

DR WILLIAMS: Mr Bowers is a good man whom I like but I feel I need to be undisturbed for a while in the house. I need to be alone to think.

(The sounds of the cab coming to a halt is heard. He coughs violently)

The fog which has been threatening on and off for the past couple of days now begins to descend in thick swirls of grey green coils. I feel the poisonous air tickling at my lungs as I breathe.

(Sounds of the cab moving off, growing fainter. A church clock chimes)

Twelve o'clock yet fog makes has darkened the light so much that already it feels as if night is closing in. There must be a thousand people within a few yards of me yet I feel alone. Alone in the fog. I pass by the entrance to the churchyard. Some instinct makes me look inside. Some instinct makes me look towards my brother's grave.

(Tinkle of tension music. Lights show the dim outline of a man in the fog. He has his back to Dr Williams)

A man. There. There by the grave.

(Doctor Williams walks uncertainly forward. Tension music rises)

Can it be Mr Bowers? Mr Bowers?

(He moves slightly nearer the figure)

No. Not Bowers. But someone familiar. I feel I know the man at the graveside.

(He coughs painfully and takes a moment to recover)

The man doesn't respond to the sound of my coughing.

You, sir. Can I help you? Sir? Are you…were you a friend of my brother's?

(As he moves towards the figure at the graveside it sinks into the mist and shadow and disappears. The music fades. Dr Williams wipes his brow and rubs his chest)

No. No. No one I know A fancy of my imagination. Yet I was certain I knew him. The chill. The fog. The strain. All must have brought on a mild fever. I saw someone at a grave. In this light I must have misjudged the distance. He was probably not at Robert's grave at all. The poor fellow, he must have taken to his heels when I bawled at him like a madman. Who could blame him? No one. No one.

(He is racked by a severe cough. He puts his handkerchief to his mouth. He checks the handkerchief)

No blood. But my lungs won't stand too much of this atmosphere. Already I feel the familiar burning when I breathe. My heart flutters and then settles into a steady rhythm once more. Suddenly out the mist, the house looms before me. Shapeless. Brooding. I pride myself on being a rational man yet despite this every sense in my being tells me to turn from here. Tells me to leave this place. But for love of my brother I will solve this mystery. I approach the gate and step inside.

(The sound of the gates creaking open is heard)

The garden. It's made even more nightmarish by the mist which turns every twisted branch into a fearful waiting…thing.

(Over the sound system echoes the brief snatch of rapid indistinct whispering of many voices)

Voices. From outside. The fog plays tricks with sounds.

(He moves forward a little)

There. By the tree. A darkness. Shaping itself out of the very air. It's not a human form as such, yet it seems more like a human than not.

(The brief despairing wail of a woman echoes. He turns quickly to the sound)

The cry. A woman. Such despair. From one of the dens of ill-repute no doubt. They are dotted around the area. That's what it is. The cry of some poor creature being abused in one of those sad houses. The shape. By the tree. It's stays for a moment and then dissolves in the air. Imagination, that's all. The shadows and the fog. I'm a scientist and I will not allow my reason to be fuddled by silly thoughts. Everything is to be explained by some agency as mortal as myself.

(He shivers and pulls his coat around him)

Cold. So cold.

As Doctor Williams is speaking in the distance the shadowy figure of the man in the graveyard appears. His face is indistinct. He silently watches Doctor Williams who is unaware of his presence. Doctor Williams stands still for a few seconds. Some sixth sense tells him of the figure's presence. The mysterious figure fades back into the fog and shadow. Doctor Williams slowly turns and looks towards the spot where the man stood. He makes as if to move towards the place and then changes his mind. He turns and walks towards the house. Fade to black.

Light up on Mr Bower's sitting in his office. He reads a note. The doctor's voice is heard in voice over.

DOCTOR WILLIAMS IN VO: My Dear Mr Bowers, Forgive the slight change in plans. Instead of meeting you at your office as we agreed I have decided to travel down to the house earlier and will rendezvous with you there at your convenience.

Yours,

Jack Williams.

MR BOWERS: On his own. Oh dear. This will not do. This will not do.

(He pulls his coat on and bawls off to his clerk)

Nesbit. Run down and hail a hansom cab. Quick as you can, sir. The matter is urgent. Very urgent.

(He begins to exit. Comes back, pours and drinks a glass of brandy. He starts to exit again. Fade down light on Bowers office. Bring light up on Doctor Williams who stands in the house which is as before.

DOCTOR WILLIAMS: The house is still in the same gloom as before. The shutters have not yet been removed from the windows. Visibility is poor and isn't helped by the tendrils of fog which have even managed to creep in here. Perhaps it's my imagination, or perhaps it's the beginning of a slight fever but it feels even colder in here than outside. A deep, bone-numbing chill. Before I go through my brother's belongings I will take a look around the house. I don't really know what I'm looking for but perhaps I'll find something, anything which will suggest what might have led to his death.

(Light up on Mr Bowers who is talking to an unseen cab driver)

MR BOWERS: Cabby. Limehouse, quick as you like. There's guinea in it for you if you get me there in double time.

(Fade down on Mr Bowers. The sound of the cab is heard for a few seconds before fading away. The church clock sounds faintly)

DR WILLIAMS: The quarter of the hour. Is it really only fifteen minutes since I stepped from the hansom cab? Even time seems to have slowed in the fog.

(He moves forward)

The kitchen bare and dust-ridden. Here on the table, a piece of bread and some cheese. Hard and dried out. This must have been Robert's. This perhaps was my brother's last meal. Eaten here in the gloom and dreariness of this place.

(There is the sound of the quick pattering of feet)

Hey! Hey! Is there someone there? Nothing. Rats perhaps. Or my senses playing tricks again. Is it my fancy or is it getting darker? No, no darker. Blacker. Not an absence of light more a gathering of darkness.

(The pattering of feet is heard again and he looks around nervously)

I fight down an irrational impulse to suddenly run madly up the stairs and out of this place but I resist. I am not a child. I have long ceased to fear the dark. Yet it's with some relief I see the comforting shape of a Bullseye on the table. Perhaps left by one of the workmen.

(He picks up the small electric lamp and turns it on)

The little pool of light restores me. I feel my courage return.

(The sound of a hansom cab is heard. Light up on Mr Bowers who calls up to an unseen driver)

MR BOWERS: What's that, driver? Yes, I know there's a fog sir. But good God, get a move on. This is a matter of some urgency.

(Fade down light on Mr Bowers. Fade down cab sounds)

DR WILLIAMS: The wine cellars, cobwebbed and dusty. I notice that a few bottles of wine are still left in the bin. There's even a bottle or two of very good brandy. Mr Bowers has obviously not been down here.

(The sound of hurried indistinct whispering is heard again)

I move out of the cellar. There's nothing to be learned down here I fear.

(The sound of soft breathing echoes over the sound system)

The bathroom where…. I don't know what to expect. Signs of the madhouse? Blood splashed walls? No, the place is as ordered and neat as Robert has always been. His shaving mug. Tooth powder. Towels.

(The soft breathing echoes more loudly)

All signs of a man in control of himself. A man who would not take his own life. What then caused my brother's death? *Who* caused my brother's death?

(He suddenly shouts at the empty house)

I will find whoever did this? Do you hear me? I will find whoever did this!

(The soft breathing halts and there is silence. Dr Williams stands silently in the gloom for a few seconds. The darkness becomes deeper and the little pool of light thrown out by the Bullseye seems frailer. He walks towards the main room again)

Back in the main drawing room I look around. Perhaps I should now start to examine my brother's belongings. Mr Bowers will expect me to have made a start.

(As he starts to look into one of the packing cases he picks up the charred diary again)

The fragment of diary.

(Over the sound system echoes the woman's voice mingling with that of Dr Williams)

DOCTOR WILLIAMS/WOMAN ON SOUND SYSTEM: We ought to love...if all was known...

DOCTOR WILLIAMS: The mysterious words of from the diary. They suddenly come unbidden to my mind. Why? Why do I remember some words which mean nothing?

(He looks at the floor. Mood music)

How strange. Fresh footprints. A child's bare footprints here on the floor. They were not here when I arrived today. At least I don't believe they were. Some local urchin perhaps came in while I was downstairs.

(As he speaks he follows the footprints. Mood music heightens)

They stop here. In the middle of the room.

(The music stops)

The child must have leapt forward. Jumped ahead.

(He searches)

But there's no sign of them resuming. This is ridiculous. Footprints can't just stop. The floor is thick with dust. How could...? This is... No, there is a rational explanation. Some trick has been played. I'm sure I shall solve the puzzle by and by. The chill is by now making my teeth chatter. For the sake of my health I don't believe I should stay here much longer. Yet I've told Mr Bower's I'll meet him.

(He lifts the Bullseye and attempts to peer around the room)

What a miserable place. I can't help but think of Robert spending his last days here. There, in the corner of the room. A door which I haven't noticed. The darkness of the walls and the gloom have almost hidden it. Only the shaft of light from the Bullseye catching the frame makes it visible.

(Bring up light on Mr Bowers. He shouts up at the unseen cab driver)

MR BOWERS: Driver! Driver! Why have we stopped now? A cart overturned you say?

(He peers ahead as if looking out of the window of the cab)

Can we go some other way? Right! Never mind. Damn! Damn! Damn!

(He takes a coin from his pocket)

Take this.

(He passes it up to the driver)

I'll make my own way from here.

(Fade down)

DR WILLIAMS: *(Moves towards the door. The sound of a door creaking open slowly is heard. Mood music)* The door. It's opened of its own accord. The pressure of me walking on the warped floorboards no doubt. With the door wide open all I can see is the darkness beyond. I should look inside. That is why I'm here. Perhaps I could wait for Mr Bowers? Or until the workmen come to take down the shutters and let some light in here? These are excuses for children. I will go into that room.

(He exits. Bring up light on Mr Bowers who gasps for breath. He takes a swig of brandy)

MR BOWERS: Nearly there. Nearly there. Dear God. Dear God. Please make me just an old fool who starts at shadows. Make the good doctor safe.

(Fade down on Mr Bowers. Light up on Dr Williams who stands in a void of darkness apart from the little pool of light thrown out by the Bullseye)

A small, blank dreary room. No furniture. A few empty boxes and old hamper.

(He shines the lamp upwards)

There's a little window set high in the wall but it's shuttered. No fireplace. No other entrance or exit apart from the way I came in.

(The rapid indistinct whispers are heard again. He spins around to find their source)

Perhaps it's my imagination again but the blackness in this room seems almost solid. Darkness is a passive thing, the absence of light. But here it seems…tangible.

(As he sweeps the room with the light beam for a millisecond the light catches the white and terrible blood-drenched face of a man. Dr Williams emits an involuntary cry of fear. Music sting)

Jesus! Oh. Oh. Oh.

(He gasps for breath)

Je…Je…Je…

(He backs up slowly. He shines the light to try and see the face again. There is no sign of the bloody figure)

Nothing. Nothing. Nothing. A trick of the light. Overheated imagination. That's all.

(The brief despairing wail of a woman echoes)

Must get some air. Can't breathe.

(He clutches at his chest)

Can't breathe.

(The sound of the door creaking slowly closed is heard)

The door. Closed.

(He tries to open the door)

Jammed. Won't move.

(He starts to pound at the door)

Ahoy. Mr Bowers? Anybody? I'm in here. The door seems to be jammed.

(The faint crying of children echoes. Suddenly the light from the Bullseye begins to fade)

Oh, no. The light. It's fading.

(Mingling with the children's crying is the terrified screams of a woman. The light from the lamp is now almost gone. Dr Williams stands in the almost pitch blackness. He shakes the lamp frantically)

Come on come on come on.

(As the light finally fades he is plunged into complete darkness. He pounds on the door)

Let me out! Let me out! Let me out!!!

End of Act One.

ACT TWO

Sound of a public house. Lights up to reveal Dr Williams and Mr Bowers sitting at a table having a drink. Dr Williams is obviously very shaken and drinks deeply.

MR BOWERS: Feeling better now, Doctor Williams?

DOCTOR WILLIAMS: Yes. Yes, much better thank you, Mr Bowers.

MR BOWERS: Good. Good. I must confess when I heard your shouts I thought the worst for a moment. I thought you were being attacked by some ruffians.

DOCTOR WILLIAMS: No. No attack. I just panicked for a few seconds when the light failed and the door jammed. I apologise for my foolish behaviour.

MR BOWERS: The door, yes. That was strange. The door. You being unable to open it, I mean. Yet I barely touched the handle and it swung open.

DOCTOR WILLIAMS: Yes. A quirk of the warped floorboards, obviously.

MR BOWERS: Obviously.

DOCTOR WILLIAMS: Your tone suggests you think otherwise, Mr Bowers.

MR BOWERS: Me? No, I'm sure you're right. It's just that...

DOCTOR WILLIAMS: It's just that?

MR BOWERS: Oh, nothing, sir, nothing at all.

DOCTOR WILLIAMS: Please, if you have some thoughts on the matter I'd like to hear them.

MR BOWERS: If you'll forgive me for saying so, Doctor Williams, your cries suggested a fear beyond merely being locked in. You sounded like a man in mortal terror.

DOCTOR WILLIAMS: Mortal terror? You speak like a writer of Penny Dreadfuls, Mr Bowers. Mortal terror of what? A jammed door handle?

MR BOWERS: Perhaps you're right. Penny Dreadfuls.

(He takes a drink of brandy)

I would urge one thing on you, however, Doctor Williams.

DOCTOR WILLIAMS: And that is?

MR BOWERS: Please don't wander around that house alone again. Give me a couple of days and I'll arrange for some workmen to open the place properly. Take the shutters down, have plenty of lamps. You and I can go through your brother's things together. In fact there's no real reason why you should have to bother going down to the house at all. I can have everything crated up and sent to a warehouse in the city. You can check the goods at your leisure.

(There is silence for a couple of seconds. Mr Bowers drains his glass and looks around the pub)

Very lively public house this. Yes, very lively. Shall we have another...?

(He indicates with his glass)

DOCTOR WILLIAMS: Tell me, Mr Bowers, why is it you seem most anxious that I don't go back to the house?

MR BOWERS: Anxious that you...? No, I'm not anxious that you... Very well, if you want the truth I would be glad of neither you or I had to set foot in that damned place again.

DOCTOR WILLIAMS: And why is that?

MR BOWERS: There's something very wrong.

DOCTOR WILLIAMS: Something wrong. What you mean ghosts and ghouls?

MR BOWERS: Something.

DOCTOR WILLIAMS: Mr Bowers, we're both educated men. Are you seriously telling me you believe in ghosts?

MR BOWERS: That's not what I said, but how do you explain the numbing cold. The noises. The locked room. The lamp going out?

DOCTOR WILLIAMS: The place is beside the river, the air will naturally be colder. The noises? Rats. People outside. A freak of acoustics. The lamp? A damp battery. As for the locked room, I told you, the house is old, the wood is warped. A twisted floorboard jammed the door shut. You trod on the board, the wood shifted. Voila, the door opens.

MR BOWERS: And you really believe that?

DOCTOR WILLIAMS: I'll tell you what I do believe, Mr Bowers, I believe that the supernatural is impossible. And what is called the supernatural is only something in the laws of nature of which we have been hitherto ignorant. Now I don't know for a fact that my explanation of the things you mentioned is absolutely correct, but it is based on rational, logical and verifiable reasoning. Do you not agree?

MR BOWERS: I think perhaps we'd better be going. The fog is thick and we may have difficulty getting a hansom cab.

DOCTOR WILLIAMS: Forgive me if appear rather dogmatic, Mr Bowers, it's the scientist in me. I hope you understand.

MR BOWERS: Of course.

DOCTOR WILLIAMS: One thing that does puzzle me, though.

MR BOWERS: That is?

DOCTOR WILLIAMS: The blank room.

MR BOWERS: The blank room?

DOCTOR WILLIAMS: Yes, the little room I was trapped in. Did you notice the odd geometry of the place?

MR BOWERS: The geometry? I'm not with you.

DOCTOR WILLIAMS: The dimensions, didn't they seem...stunted? Not quite right?

MR BOWERS: No, I can't say I noticed, although I've barely looked at the room properly.

DOCTOR WILLIAMS: For instance, the window high up. It was nearer the back wall than one would have thought. Who would place a window so close to one side of a room?

MR BOWERS: I don't really know. Maybe there's some structural reason the window had to be put there.

DOCTOR WILLIAMS: Perhaps. I do agree with you that something is 'wrong' in that house. But I believe whatever it is has human origins. And it contributed to my brother's death. I am determined to go back there and investigate further. I will find out the truth about Robert one way or another.

(There is a beat as Mr Bowers looks at Dr Williams)

MR BOWERS: I told you the place has a history, Doctor Williams, if you are determined to look further into your brother's death then if you can call at my office tomorrow morning, shall we say at ten, then I have some facts pertaining to the house which you may find interesting.

DOCTOR WILLIAMS: Can't you tell me now?

MR BOWERS: Forgive me, Doctor Williams, but you look in a rather bad state. It would be better if you had a good night's sleep. What I have to tell you can wait a little while longer.

DOCTOR WILLIAMS: Did my brother know these 'facts', Mr Bowers?

MR BOWERS: No. No. I only learned of then after his death. Though I just wish to God I had been able to tell him earlier. Perhaps he might be alive today.

(Fade to black. The sounds of the public house die away. Sounds of a grandfather clock striking. Light up on a chair in Dr Williams' study. An ill and feverish Dr Williams enters.. He is in a fit of coughing and struggles for breath until the fit subsides. He sits down)

DOCTOR WILLIAMS: Sleep is once again impossible. My lungs are becoming inflamed. This weather. If I remain here too much longer the damage may become irreparable. I have the beginnings of a fever. The fog has now become a real 'pea-souper' and presses against the windows making me feel as if I'm sealed in a tomb. Thoughts, such wild thoughts. I will bring reason to this mystery. I must bring reason! The facts. A house vacated for five years. The tenants who have tried to live there have left almost immediately. Robert spends three days in the house and dies there. I've experienced the strange noises and odd things which happen, but unlike others who've fled the place I don't believe in the supernatural. Everything which happens has a logical cause. As a man of science, this I know! And I know too that my brother would have seen any unexplained phenomena in the same light. He was scientist. Bogie men and ghosties were not something to scare him. Robert would not have had an attack of the vapours at every creaking floorboard.

(He coughs and takes a few seconds to recover)

What do I deduce from this? If I start from the premise that all the strangeness about that house is derived from a natural source then it follows that perhaps there is a human agency behind it. Is there something in the house that some person, or persons, need to protect? Are the noises and voices just to keep people away? Was my brother murdered because he refused to be scared off? And if so, for what reason? Whatever the explanation it led to my brother's death. I will find the cause if I have to pull down that house brick by brick.

(Fade down on Dr Williams Light up on Mr Bowers office. He sits reading. Dr Williams enters. He looks very ill)

MR BOWERS: Ah, good morning Doctor Williams, I…My God, man! You look terrible!

DOCTOR WILLIAMS: Thank you. My morale has just risen by leaps and bounds.

MR BOWERS: Sit down. Sit down.

(Dr Williams sits heavily in the seat)

MR BOWERS: Doctor Williams, forgive my presumptuousness but I think you should be in bed and not walking the streets in this weather. Let me send for a cab. We'll have you back home safe and snug in no time.

DOCTOR WILLIAMS: No. Please. I'm fine. Fine. Just a little inflammation of the chest. I'll be alright by and by.

MR BOWERS: Shall I send for a doctor?

DOCTOR WILLIAMS: You have one on the premises. What is it they say? "Physician heal thyself". On the way here I had a chemist mix me a prescription. I should feel the effects quite soon. So, please, don't disturb yourself, Mr Bowers.

MR BOWERS: Well at least have a drop of brandy to warm the cockles.

(He pours a glass of brandy and then another)

Oops, Silly me. I've poured two glasses. Never mind.

(He checks the glasses besides each other and hands the smaller amount to Dr Williams) Here you are, sir.

DR WILLIAMS: Thank you.

(He takes a drink and coughs slightly)

MR BOWERS: Better?

DOCTOR WILLIAMS: Yes. Thank you.

MR BOWERS: Your health.

(He drinks the brandy)

DOCTOR WILLIAMS: You said last night you had some facts about the house which might be relevant to my brother's death.

MR BOWERS: Well, I don't know about being directly relevant to his death, Doctor Williams. I meant I'm aware of certain events that might throw a light the strange history of the house. This is no way constitutes...

DOCTOR WILLIAMS: Mr Bowers! No lawyers equivocations. Just tell me what you know of the house. Please.

MR BOWERS: When I attended your brother's inquest I met, quite by chance, an old friend, a police inspector from Scotland Yard. He was as surprised to see me as I was him. We went for a drink afterwards. He told me, in strict confidence of course, that the police had conducted enquiries in that house some five years before.

DOCTOR WILLIAMS: Enquiries?

MR BOWERS: Yes. You remember I said that the original owners had left the house five years previously, and since then it has been almost impossible to keep tenants?

DOCTOR WILLIAMS: I remember. But what has this to do with the police?

MR BOWERS: The owner of that house was...is... a sea captain. A man apparently of brutal temperament. There were rumours that he'd once beaten a member of his crew to death and thrown him overboard. Nothing was proven, of course. Well, he married. His new wife was just a slip of a girl. Almost twenty five years younger than him. A gentle, pretty little woman, it seems. Given away, sold really, by parents who saw the opportunity to hook a rich son-in-law even if it meant riding roughshod over their daughter's wishes.

DOCTOR WILLIAMS: I don't see....

MR BOWERS: Please. Your indulgence. Well, the inevitable happened. The poor girl was shackled to a brute who put her through cruelties we probably find hard to imagine.

(Over the sound system echoes a woman's screams of terror. The sound of blows being rained down are heard)

It's said her cries could be heard for half a mile when he was back home and drunk.

DOCTOR WILLIAMS: And nothing was done?

MR BOWERS: What could be done? A wife is her husband's property to do with as he wishes. Unless he'd killed actually killed the poor woman the law would stand aside. In space of a few years there were two children of the marriage. A boy and a girl. Not that the arrival of children mellowed the captain. It just meant more souls to terrorise.

(Over the sound system echoes the screams of a woman mingling with the cries of children saying "No, father, no")

Those poor little innocents. At the mercy of a beast and only their mother stood between them and him. From what neighbours said she'd often appear battered

41

and bruised. Trying to keep her dignity. Trying to act as if all was well. The children clung to her skirts and were afraid of speaking to anyone.

(The sounds of the screams and cries fade away)

After her husband had left for a particularly long voyage the children caught the croup and she sent for a doctor. The doctor was young. He was kind. He began to call regularly at the house. Tongues began to wag.

(Waltz music is heard echoing. A woman and man's laughter mingle)

It was if they didn't care. They became bolder and bolder. Walking in public. Arm in arm. The children laughing by their sides.

(Slowly the dance music become discordant)

They were living in a fool's paradise, of course. The captain returned sooner than expected. He didn't catch them in flagrante, so to speak, but the gossip was rife.

(The discordant music fades away)

DOCTOR WILLIAMS: Did he harm them?

MR BOWERS: The man was cruel for its own sake. What do you think he did with a reason for hurting her?

(Over the sound system echoes the screams of a woman, the wailing of children and the sound of blows. A man's voice is heard shouting "Whore, whore, filthy whore".

The sounds fade away)

DOCTOR WILLIAMS: And the young doctor?

MR BOWERS: Walked out of his surgery and never returned.

DOCTOR WILLIAMS: Sad.

MR BOWERS: Yes.

DOCTOR WILLIAMS: What happened to the captain and his family?

MR BOWERS: Well, a few weeks after the doctor left the captain put the place up for rent. He said they were leaving for America. He sent the unfortunate wife and children on ahead, tidied up his affairs and put the house in the hands of a factor to be let. Apparently all correspondence is forwarded to an address in San Francisco.

DOCTOR WILLIAMS: So why were the police interested in all this? You said the law saw it as a domestic matter.

MR BOWERS: Ah, that was apparently at the instigation of the doctor's family. The young man came from influential stock. When he failed to contact them for several weeks they got in touch with Scotland Yard. That's where my friend the inspector came in. He was assigned to investigate. As I said, it was from him I learned all this.

DOCTOR WILLIAMS: Did they trace the doctor?

MR BOWERS: No. It was thought that he wanted to place as much distance between himself and the captain.

DOCTOR WILLIAMS: And could the young wife or the captain throw no light on his whereabouts?

MR BOWERS: Gone. All of them. By the time the police investigation had begun they had left for America.

DOCTOR WILLIAMS: But surely the police didn't just leave things at that!

MR BOWERS What else could be done? It's not a crime for a man to disappear. There was no evidence of anything remiss. And to be honest I wouldn't blame him for leaving without trace. It's obvious the captain wasn't a man to cross.

DOCTOR WILLIAMS: So, the doctor has never been seen again?

MR BOWERS: Not to my knowledge, although it's possible he's done so since the police completed their enquiries.

DOCTOR WILLIAMS: Do you think he could have followed the captain and his family to America? Tried to resume his love affair?

MR BOWERS: I doubt it. If he did he was a braver man than me. As I said the captain was…fearsome.

DOCTOR WILLIAMS: Strange story. And the police never tried to contact the captain and his family in America?

MR BOWERS: Why would they do that?

DOCTOR WILLIAMS: No reason, I suppose.

MR BOWERS: Since then the house has been the subject of every fantastical neighbourhood tale you can imagine, from being haunted to containing buried treasure.

DOCTOR WILLIAMS: Buried treasure?

MR BOWERS: Oh, more nonsense. Local gossip. People said the captain had hidden money around the house, money he made illegally. The rumours said he intended to return and claim it when it was safe to do so. For the first couple of weeks after they left the place was ransacked by every half-wit in east London looking for this supposed 'hidden treasure' Needless to say nothing was found.

DOCTOR WILLIAMS: You said last night that if my brother had known of these facts he might be alive today. What did you mean by that?

MR BOWERS: Forgive me, I was perhaps being a little too fanciful, Doctor Williams. I only meant that had your brother been more aware of the house's...dubious history, he might well have been less keen to take it on. I still regret not being in possession of those facts before I allowed him to proceed.

DOCTOR WILLIAMS: Rest your mind on that point, Mr Bowers. Not one jot of what you've told me would have swayed Robert in any way. I'm certain he would have carried on with his plans anyway.

MR BOWERS: Thank you for that. It eases my mind considerably, sir. Now, is there anything else I can do for you or shall we arrange to travel down to the house when the workmen finally take down the shutters, and we can see things properly?

DOCTOR WILLIAMS: There is one thing.

MR BOWERS: Yes?

DOCTOR WILLIAMS: Do you have a plan of the property?

MR BOWERS: A plan? Yes, yes, I believe we do. We obtained a copy when your brother was deciding the alterations.

DOCTOR WILLIAMS: May I see the drawing?

MR BOWERS: See it? Yes, of course. Excuse me.

(He exits. As he does so he calls to his clerk)

Nesbit. Look out the plans for the Limehouse property, will you?

DOCTOR WILLIAMS: I feel weak and feverish yet strangely elated. The story of the house has given me the glimmerings of a theory about what may be at the bottom of all this.

(He coughs. It becomes a spasm which racks him. He puts a handkerchief to his mouth to stifle the cough. When he takes the handkerchief away there are a few spots of blood to be seen)

The consumption has returned. I also feel my heart suddenly palpitating and then slowing again. If I stay in London for much longer it will be a death sentence. Yet I will find out who or what is responsible for my brother's death.

(Over the sound system comes echoes a woman's voice)

WOMAN ON SOUND SYSTEM: We ought to love....if all was known.

DOCTOR WILLIAMS: The diary. Those strange words. In my mind again. The hidden thoughts of the captain's young wife, perhaps? In that little locked diary did she reveal the secrets of her heart?

(He coughs again, this time less violently. Mr Bowers enters with the house plan. Dr Williams hurriedly composes himself)

MR BOWERS: Alright, Doctor Williams?

DOCTOR WILLIAMS: Fine. Fine. Just a tickle in the throat. You have the plan, good man.

(The plan is opened out on the table before them. Doctor Williams studies it carefully)

MR BOWERS: I also have a copy of the changes proposed by you brother, if you'd like to see them.

DOCTOR WILLIAMS: What? No. No thank you, Mr Bowers, that won't be necessary.

(He jabs his finger on the plan)

Yes. Yes. I thought so. I thought so.

MR BOWERS: Thought what?

DOCTOR WILLIAMS: Maybe an answer to this mystery.

(He grabs the plan)

Mr Bowers, come with me if you please.

(He exits)

MR BOWERS: Doctor Williams. Where are we going? The answer to what mystery? Doctor Williams? Doctor Williams?

(He exits in pursuit. Fade down light on the office. The shadow of a stained glass window is splashed across the stage. Dr Williams kneels as if in prayer.

DOCTOR WILLIAMS: The church is deadly cold. The air smells of dankness and incense. Near the altar a few candles gutter feebly. The pews are polished by the bodies of a hundred years of worship. Mr Bowers has gone to the Chandlers shop at my request. I'll meet him at the house. Why am I here? Here in this church? Just outside my brother lies in the dark, damp ground. He wasn't a believer in anything but science. No gods or demons. No ghosts. No heaven. No hell. Neither do I, yet I feel compelled to come here for some sort of comfort before I enter the house.

(As he speaks the mysterious man from before is seen hidden in the shadows, his back almost to Doctor Williams. Mood music)

Maybe I'm a coward. The great man of science who clings to the rituals of faith the moment his courage is tested. I just need...I just need more than learning before I go back to that place. I need more than facts and reason to take with me. I know that the root of this mystery lies in the laws of nature but I...

(He turns slowly to see the mysterious figure. Mood music rises)

The man. The same man from the graveyard. I know him. I *know* I know him!

(He walks slowly towards the figure)

You, sir. Wait there. A word if you please.

(The mysterious figure turns slightly toward Dr Williams although his face is still obscured)

No! No! This can't...Robert? Robert?

(The music stops. He covers his face with his hands. The figure fades away into the shadows)

Am I going mad? It looked like...no...it was Robert. It was my dead brother! Help me. Somebody. Anybody. God. If there is a God. Prove yourself now. One sign. One proof. That's all. That's all it needs. Come on, God. One scientist to another. Show me! Show me! Show me!!!

(He pulls himself together with a supreme effort of will and takes several deep breaths)

Stupid. Stupid. There's an explanation. Of course there is. The fever. Exhaustion. Strain. Grief. Worry. All combining. All combining to play tricks on my senses. I must be strong. I must keep my nerves in check. Only for another hour or so. For it's then I believe I shall have solved the mystery of that house once and for all.

(Fade down on Dr Williams. Light up on Mr Bowers who stands in the house grounds. Fog swirls thickly around. He holds a crowbar in his hand. The melancholy boom of a ship's horn is heard. Mr Bowers looks about nervously and then takes a swig from his hip flask. As he does so Dr Williams enters. He carries the house plans)

DOCTOR WILLIAMS: Mr Bowers.

(His sudden appearance startles Mr Bowers causing the brandy to go down the wrong way. He coughs and splutters and gasps loudly as he tries to regain his breath)

Are you alright?

(Mr Bowers nods that he'll be alright while fighting noisily for air)

Are you sure?

(Mr Bowers again nods)

Well, take your time

MR BOWERS: I'm…I'm fine…fine. *(His voice is strangulated and hoarse)*

DOCTOR WILLIAMS: It's just as I suspected. The measurements of the blank room doesn't tally with those on the plans.

MR BOWERS: Is that important?

DOCTOR WILLIAMS: You remember I said that the proportions of the blank room felt…stunted?

MR BOWERS: Yes, but I still don't see….

DOCTOR WILLIAMS: I paced the distance from the front door to the back wall of that room, and there's eight feet missing.

MR BOWERS: Missing? How can a room have eight feet missing?

DOCTOR WILLIAMS: Exactly. I wondered why the window was jammed up against the back wall in that odd way. But the reason's obvious now

MR BOWERS: Of course. What's obvious?

DOCTOR WILLIAMS: The wall is false. The real wall is eight feet further back.

MR BOWERS: But why should anyone want to make a room eight feet smaller?

DOCTOR WILLIAMS: Why indeed, but I think we'll find out.

MR BOWERS: Dr Williams, there must be a hundred reasons why the interior wall doesn't tally with the plans.

DR WILLIAMS: Such as?

MR BOWERS: Oh, well…eh…perhaps the back part of the room was used as storage space.

DR WILLIAMS: Mr Bowers, I saw the back wall, it's blank. No doors.

MR BOWERS: Then perhaps the room was too large for their requirements.

(Dr Williams gives him a look of incredulity)

Oh, well, I know that doesn't sound plausible but there surely must be a perfectly simple and logical explanation.

DR WILLIAMS: Well, if there is, we'll find it, Mr Bowers.

MR BOWERS: Find it? How do you mean?

(Dr takes the crowbar from Mr Bowers)

DR WILLIAMS: With this.

MR BOWERS: You don't mean…? Oh, no, I'm sorry, Doctor Williams. That will not do, sir, that will not do at all.

DR WILLIAMS: Why do you think I asked you fetch it then, Mr Bowers?

MR BOWERS: To open the packing cases of course. I never thought… I'm afraid I can't permit this, Doctor Williams. I can't collude in the damage of this property.

DR WILLIAMS: I assure you I'll pay for any damage.

MR BOWERS: That's not the point, Doctor. You see…

DR WILLIAMS: My brother died here and I want to know why. That's *the point.*

(He exits into house)

MR BOWERS: Doctor Williams. Doctor Williams. Wait. Wait.

(Fade down on Mr Bowers as he exits In the darkness the rapid and indistinct whispering of many voices echoes for a few seconds and then fades away. Light up inside the house as before. Tendrils of fog drifts around. Doctor Williams holds the crowbar in one hand and a bullseye lamp in the other. He lets the beam play around the room. Enter Mr Bowers)

MR BOWERS: Doctor Williams, I really do insist that we leave this to another day.

DR WILLIAMS: What other day?

MR BOWERS: Well, look at the place for a start. Hardly any light. Fog creeping around, and you know what that can do to your health, Doctor Williams. Listen, I understand your need to find a reason for your brother's death. It's natural. But this isn't the way to go about it. Tell you what we'll do, we'll go back to town. I'll contact the builder and in the morning we'll come down here with half a dozen navvies and tear down that wall in two ticks, how's that? In fact we could...

(The sound of children wailing echoes briefly)

DR WILLIAMS: Ssshh. Did you hear that?

MR BOWERS: Hear what?

DR WILLIAMS: The crying. Children crying.

MR BOWERS: No, I can't say that I...

(A woman's wail echoes briefly)

DR WILLIAMS: You must have heard that!

MR BOWERS: I promise you I can't...

DR WILLIAMS: Children, crying. And a woman in pain, fear.

MR BOWERS: Doctor Williams, I didn't hear anything. There were no cries.

DR WILLIAMS: *(He stares into the shadows. He points)* There. Do you see *that*, sir?

MR BOWERS: For heavens sake what?

DR WILLIAMS: In the corner, there's someone...something there.

(He begins to walk slowly towards the shadows. Tinkle of tension music. He shines the bullseye)

MR BOWERS: Are you sure?

DR WILLIAMS: Have you no eyes? I saw something. It's shape against the light.

(They both move slowly almost to the shadows. Tension music gets louder and louder till it reaches a crescendo. Suddenly Mr Bowers emits a terrified scream and stamps wildly on the floor)

MR BOWERS: Rats. Rats. Filthy rats.

(He stamps a few times more and then moves away to the centre of the room again. He's distraught and drinks mightily from his hip flask while Dr Williams peers into the gloom and then re-joins him)

DR WILLIAMS: Are you alright, Mr Bowers?

MR BOWERS: Yes, yes, thank you. Filthy things. Filthy.

(He raises his flask to his lips and then proffers it to Dr Williams)

Would you....?

DR WILLIAMS: No thank you.

MR BOWERS: Well, at least we know what noises you heard, Doctor Williams. Filthy, stinking rats.

DR WILLIAMS: What I h...he...he...

(He coughs violently)

Wha...wha...

(He coughs again before slowly regaining his breath)

What I heard and saw was not rats, Mr Bowers.

MR BOWERS: Oh, for heaven's sake, man, what else could it be, ghosts? Things that go bump in the night?

DR WILLIAMS: I told you, I don't believe in anything that can't be explained by science.

MR BOWERS: And what does science tell you is making things happen, if not rats?

DR WILLIAMS: I don't know exactly but whatever it is, Mr Bowers, it has a natural origin. Perhaps someone is trying to discourage us from staying around.

MR BOWERS: But why would anyone do that?

DR WILLIAMS: You remember you told me people believed the captain had hidden money here?

MR BOWERS: Yes. But that was just street gossip.

DR WILLIAMS: Perhaps, but maybe someone believes it to be true all the same.

MR BOWERS: I don't follow you?

DR WILLIAMS: Suppose there's people who think the money *is* here, then it's in their interests to make sure nobody else is around while they search. Right? Somebody so desperate they'd kill to keep people away? My brother wasn't one to be frightened by noises in the dark, Mr Bowers, perhaps by murdering him and faking it to look like suicide was the only way to get rid of him.

MR BOWERS: Oh, that's too fanciful for words, Doctor.

DR WILLIAMS: Possibly but do you have any other hypothesis which fits the facts?

MR BOWERS: No, granted, but have you any real evidence to support such a theory?

DR WILLIAMS: Not at this time, but I'm sure that blank room holds some of the answers. Are you ready?

MR BOWERS: Ready?

DR WILLIAMS: To learn the truth? In the blank room?

MR BOWERS: Dr Williams, I've no intention of going within a twenty yards of that room, not now, not ever. And if you've any sense you'll leave it alone as well.

DR WILLIAMS: I won't be long, Mr Bowers.

(He makes to walk towards the blank room. Mr Bowers grabs him by the arm)

MR BOWERS: No.

DR WILLIAMS: Let go of me, if you please.

MR BOWERS: Dr Williams, look at you. You're ill, sir. Your brow is covered in sweat. You're shaking. Come back with me before it's too late.

DR WILLIAMS: I'm fine. Fine. Just a minor palpitation and a slight fever.

MR BOWERS: Then I'm asking you, begging you not to do this. For my sake if not for yours. There's something not right in this house. You must feel it yourself. Please come away with me, now. I give you my word we'll come back tomorrow with an army of builders and pull the place to the ground if you want, but leave with me now!

DR WILLIAMS: Mr Bowers, your concern is much appreciated, and I've come to think of you over the past few days as a friend, but I've got to do this now. Can't you see? The whole basis of my life is fixed upon the real world. If I wait till there's others around then I'm admitting I'm afraid of the dark. I undermine my whole outlook on life. My brother was the same. It's why he wasn't afraid to stay here. But something, something as real as you and I caused his death and I'm not leaving here till I find out what. Now, if you please, sir.

(He looks at the hold Mr Bowers has on his arm. The solicitor drops his hand away)

MR BOWERS: I'm going back to my office. Please call on me when you finish here.

DR WILLIAMS: I will. Thank you.

(He exits. Mr Bowers stands alone for a few seconds. The atmosphere causes him to shiver and he exits towards the front door. Fade to black. In the darkness can be heard the sound of thumping as Dr Williams hacks at the wall in the blank room. Lights up to reveal the doctor in the gloom. Thick shadow surrounds him. He holds the crowbar in his hand. His jacket lies on the floor. The bullseye casts a feeble glow)

DR WILLIAMS: Faint. I feel faint, but I must go on. The wall is only single brick and there's a hollow beyond as I thought. Another few blows and I should be able to start make the hole big en...

(He is racked by a violent coughing. He puts his handkerchief to his mouth. When the coughing ceases the handkerchief is filled with blood)

God. God. My lungs are haemorrhaging. Can't brea...brea...breathe...Heart is fluttering. I will go on. Must go on.

(He strikes with a frenzied desperation at the wall which is hidden in the darkness. After a few blows the terrible wail of a woman echoes)

I won't be frightened away, do you hear? I won't be frightened away!

(He strikes at the wall furiously. Suddenly the sound of the bricks collapsing is heard. He steps back)

The wall. Collapsed.

(He picks up the bullseye and peers as if into the cavity. He reels back and screams)

No! No! No! Dead. All dead. The children. The woman. A man, his skull smashed to pieces.

(The faint sound of children screaming and the woman crying echoes. The captain's voice is heard shouting 'Whore. Whore')

He killed the doctor and then...dear God he walled up his wife and children with dead body, walled them up alive. The bricks, covered with bloody marks. They tried to claw their way out with their bare hands.

(The wailing and screaming becomes louder)

There in the dark. Buried alive.

(He clutches at his chest)

Pain.

(The cries rise louder. The doctor still clutching his chest tries to make for the door. In the shadows he sees a figure)

Mr Bowers?

(As he holds the light up he sees the figure of a man his head bowed so that his face is obscured. His white shirt is drenched with blood)

Robert! Robert!

(Dr Williams sinks to his knees, gasping for breath. He feebly tries to reach out to the apparition but the blood drenched figure sinks back into the shadows)

Robert...Robert...did...did kill himself. They...they drove him to it.

(The cries and screams have reached a new height. Mingling with the cacophony is the sound of malevolent mocking laughter. The laughter and screams are now almost deafening. The doctor is on his knees, his hands over his ears trying to shut out the sounds)

Help me! In the name of Christ somebody help me!

(The wailing cries and laughter have reached a crescendo. He lets out a single despairing scream. Blackout. The noises cease instantly. There is silence and darkness for a couple of beats. A pool of light reveals a coffin on a bier. The circle

is complete and the play has returned to the setting at the start of Act One. Light up on Mr Bowers who is finishing the eulogy.

MR BOWERS: God in his infinite wisdom and mercy chose to take him from us. And so I ask you today to join me in prayer for the repose of his soul.

(He bends his head in prayer. Dr Williams enters and stands by the coffin)

DR WILLIAMS: I know now how my brother died. Driven to madness by the tortured souls who haunt the house.

(He places his hand on the coffin)

The man Mr Bowers just spoke about is me. This coffin is mine. I died in that blank room. Now I'm here, in this house… with them…for ever.

(The echoing sounds of wailing, screaming and mad laughter surrounds him as he stands as a soul lost. Fade to black. The sounds linger on the air for a few moments before dying away)

The End.

Made in the USA
San Bernardino, CA
14 December 2017